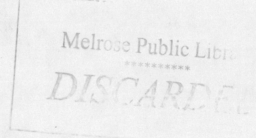

Crabapples

SUMMER CAMP

Bobbie Kalman

 Crabtree Publishing Company

Crabapples

created by Bobbie Kalman

for Eva and Zoli

Editor-in-Chief
Bobbie Kalman

Writing team
Bobbie Kalman
David Schimpky

Managing editor
Lynda Hale

Editors
Tammy Everts
Lynda Hale
April Fast

Computer design
Lynda Hale
David Schimpky

Color separations and film
Dot 'n Line Image Inc.

Printer
Worzalla Publishing Company

Special thanks to Marc Coaté at Moorelands Camp, Steven Hemming at YMCA Camp Wanakita, Marc Katz at Long Lake Camp for the Arts, Jocelyn Palm at Glen Bernard Camp, Joyce Schimpky at Camp Crossroads, and Janet Ackerley at the Easter Seals Society

Illustrations
Barb Bedell

Photographs
Joyce Schimpky/Camp Crossroads: front cover, pages 6, 8 (bottom), 14, 16 (bottom), 18 (bottom), 19 (bottom), 20 (bottom), 23 (both), 26 (bottom)
Marc Coaté/Moorelands Camp: back cover, title page, pages 7 (bottom), 8 (top), 9 (top), 12 (bottom), 17, 27, 28-29, 30, 31 (top)
Marc Crabtree: pages 10, 11, 26 (top)

Patrick H. Davies: page 12 (top)
Easter Seals Society: pages 5 (top), 9 (bottom), 31 (bottom)
Glen Bernard Camp: pages 13 (bottom), 15, 20 (top)
Bobbie Kalman: page 7 (top)
Long Lake Camp for the Arts: pages 4 (top), 5 (bottom), 19 (top), 21 (both), 22, 24 (both), 25
Don Standfield: pages 4 (bottom), 13 (top), 16 (top), 18 (top)

Crabtree Publishing Company

350 Fifth Avenue
Suite 3308
New York
N.Y. 10118

360 York Road, RR 4,
Niagara-on-the-Lake,
Ontario, Canada
L0S 1J0

73 Lime Walk
Headington
Oxford OX3 7AD
United Kingdom

Cataloging in Publication Data

Kalman, Bobbie, 1947-
Summer camp

(Crabapples)
Includes index.
ISBN 0-86505-620-X (library bound) ISBN 0-86505-720-6 (pbk.)
This book shows life at summer camp, including the daily routine and activities such as sports, performing arts, and crafts.

1. Camps - Juvenile literature. 2. Outdoor recreation - Juvenile literature. I. Title. II. Series: Kalman, Bobbie, 1947- Crabapples.

GV192.2.K35 1995   j796.54'2   LC 94-44936
                                                          CIP

What is in this book?

Camp fun

Have you ever been to summer camp? You can stay for a week, two weeks, or all summer! Every camp is different, but they have one thing in common—they are all lots of fun!

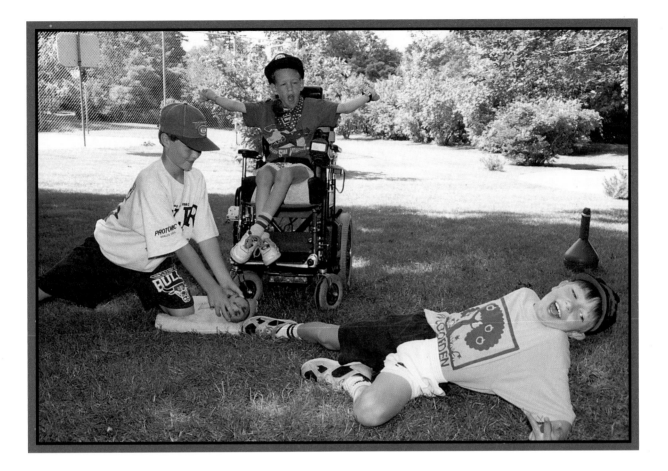

Do you enjoy the thrill of playing sports? Maybe you have some great craft ideas. Would you like to zip across the lake in a sailboat? At some camps, you can even learn to swing on a trapeze! Summer camp gives you a chance to discover your hidden talents.

Ready to go!

You don't have to worry about what to take. The camp will send you a list of everything you need to pack. You can bring a blanket or stuffed toy if you like. Other campers will have their favorite things, too.

If you are going to camp for the first time, you might feel a little scared. Maybe you haven't been away from home before. Will you like all those new kids? Will they like you?

Other children will be at the camp for the first time, too. You will have fun learning new things and making new friends.

Camp helpers

There are many people who spend the summer working at camp. They will help you have a fun time.

The camp director makes sure everything goes smoothly. Cooks prepare all your meals. The camp doctor or nurse helps campers who are sick or hurt.

The **counselors** are the people that you will get to know best. Each counselor takes care of a small group of campers. Your counselor will be your friend.

Counselors also lead camp activities, such as crafts, canoeing, and sports. Some counselors are **lifeguards**. They are in charge of the swimming area. You can learn a lot from your counselor!

Your place

Your home at camp is a tent or a cabin. You share it with a counselor and a number of other campers. Each person in the cabin sleeps in a bunk bed. Do you want the bottom or the top?

You and your cabin-mates will get to know one another well. You will go hiking, swimming, and canoeing together. You will sit together at mealtimes. Sharing secrets, playing pranks, and telling scary stories in the dark are part of cabin capers!

The cabins and tents are checked every day. It is up to you and your roommates to keep yours clean. At some camps, the cleanest cabin wins a prize. Grab a broom, a mop, and a cleaning rag—it's time to clean up this mess!

CLEANEST CABIN AWARD

A full day

The sun is up, and it's time to get going! Are you ready to exercise before breakfast? Will you take a chilly swim in the lake?

The morning is filled with activities. Do you want to go on a nature hike, or are you in the mood to make a craft?

Mmm... lunchtime! Fried chicken, spicy tacos, or hamburgers might be on the menu!

12

After supper, the whole camp takes part in games and activities. When it gets dark, you can go for a walk and look at the stars. Don't stay out too late! You'll need plenty of rest for tomorrow's activities.

Part of the afternoon is "free time." You can do whatever you like. You can sleep or read a book. Some campers write letters to their parents. Others buy snacks or souvenirs at the camp store. It is called the **tuck shop**.

Canoeing

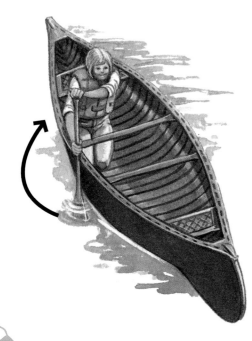

Almost every camp has canoes. Before you go canoeing, you need to learn how to use a paddle. Pulling the paddle through the water makes the canoe move.

There are different kinds of paddle strokes. One is called a **C-stroke**. Can you "C" how it got its name?

Be careful when you are in a canoe! If you stand up, your canoe might tip over. Don't worry, though. Your life jacket will help you float, and someone will come to help. The best part about canoeing is sneaking up on other canoeists and splashing them. WATER FIGHT!

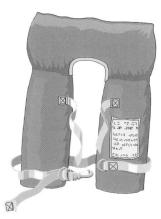

Swimming

Many people learn to swim at camp. Some campers already know how to swim, but they want to swim better. Lifeguards give swimming lessons to campers.

The lifeguard watches carefully to make sure that everyone in the water is safe. To make the lifeguard's job easier, most camps use the **buddy system**.

The buddy system is very simple. Everyone who swims has a partner called a buddy. You and your buddy must keep an eye on each other. If one buddy needs help, the other buddy calls the lifeguard.

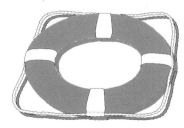

Wind sports

Windsurfing and sailing are exciting sports, but they are not easy! If you don't know what you are doing, you could end up in the water. You might even drift to the other side of the lake! Before long you will learn how to sail or windsurf. You will glide smoothly across the lake.

Water-skiing

Many campers get a chance to try water-skiing at camp. Do you think you could skim across the water on one ski?

If you don't want to water-ski, you can go for a ride in a huge tube. You may wipe out, but don't worry—even wiping out is fun!

Sports

Can you climb to the top of a rock wall? Do you know how to whack a tennis ball with a racket? Can you shoot a basketball through a hoop?

Being good at these sports takes practice and skill. At camp, you can learn to play all kinds of exciting sports.

You can do almost any craft at camp—all you need is your imagination! Tie-dye a T-shirt or build a little cabin out of popsicle sticks. Paint a picture or make a colorful necklace from beads. You can even mold a sculpture out of clay. Feel the slippery clay squish between your fingers.

Horseback riding

Have you ever wished to have your own horse? At many summer camps, you will have the chance to ride one of these beautiful animals. You can trot through forests and meadows. You might even learn to jump over a fence!

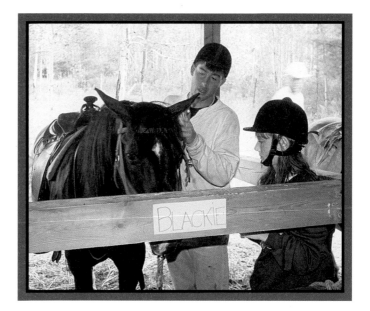

The riding instructors will show you how to take care of a horse. You can feed the horse and brush its coat.

You will also learn how the bridle and saddle are put on. Don't you wish you could take your horse home with you?

Showtime!

Do you like to sing, dance, or act? At some camps you can be in the spotlight! You can perform in a play or help make a movie using a video camera. Do you play guitar, piano, or drums? Perhaps you and some other young musicians can start your own camp band.

At some camps you can learn circus acts,
such as juggling, acrobatics, and flying
on the trapeze. At the end of summer,
you will thrill your fellow campers with
your daredevil performance.

Camping out

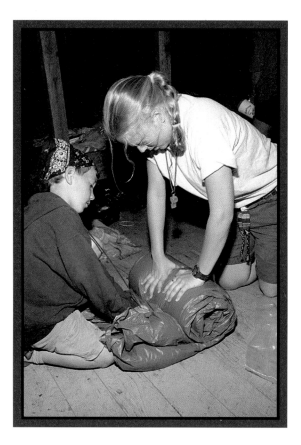

For many campers, the overnight trip is the most exciting part of camp. Before you head out, you need to pack a sleeping bag and some clothes in a waterproof bag.

You hike or canoe to the campsite and set up your tent. Soon it's time for a delicious dinner cooked over an open fire.

If you stay more than one night, you will
have time to explore the area around
your campsite. You might go on a hike or
take a canoe ride. If you are quiet, you
could spot some wild animals. In what
ways can you be a nature-friendly camper?